Original title:
Peach and Ponder

Copyright © 2025 Creative Arts Management OÜ
All rights reserved.

Author: Colin Leclair
ISBN HARDBACK: 978-1-80586-270-3
ISBN PAPERBACK: 978-1-80586-742-5

Movement of Light

A beam danced over my breakfast plate,
Chasing crumbs 'til they met their fate.
Sunny-side eggs with a wobbly flair,
Who knew photons were such a dare?

The toaster popped with a joyful shout,
Light zipped past, swirling about.
It tickled the muffins, made them rise,
As shadows giggled and waved their ties.

A flash in the fridge, snack-time delight,
Grapes in a conga line, what a sight!
They spun through the kitchen—a fruity parade,
As jars of jam cheered, "We're not afraid!"

A sunny explosion on my good old chair,
Bouncing around like it hasn't a care.
Each patch of brightness, a whimsical guest,
Making the mundane feel truly blessed.

From Branch to Muse

In the orchard, I found a hat,
A squirrel thought it was a mat.
He leaped and spun, a little show,
While I just laughed, 'Come on, let's go!'

With every bite, the juices drip,
A sticky hand, a funny slip.
The birds all chirp a jolly tune,
As thoughts swirl round like leaves in June.

Silken Thoughts in the Breeze

A breeze whispers secrets, sweet and light,
Like candy floss on a summer night.
My mind drifts up, like kites in flight,
While daisies dance, oh what a sight!

Giggles echo around the glade,
As ants march on in a silly parade.
With each soft touch, the grass gives way,
To laughter's echo, come join the play!

A Dance of Light and Shade

Sunbeams peek through the leafy veil,
Casting shadows that tell a tale.
A rabbit hops in a charming jig,
While I laugh hard, it's my kind of gig.

Leaves rustle, making a joyful sound,
As I trip lightly, not to be found.
With every step, the world's a stage,
In this silly dance, I'm free from cage!

Tasting the Quiet

In stillness, I find a ripe delight,
With flavors bursting, oh what a bite!
The world hushes, but I cannot stop,
As thoughts bounce like a playful prop.

Around me, whispers of nature play,
A chorus of chirps, come, join the fray.
With flavors tickling my funny bone,
I savor this quiet, but not alone.

The Flavor of Dreams

In a garden where giggles grow,
Fruits are swaying, don't you know?
Dancing with bees, under the sun,
Every bite's a joke, and it's all in fun.

Lemon's sour, but don't you fret,
Tickling taste buds, it's the best bet.
Jellybeans tumble, a rainbow parade,
Sweet, silly moments, never to fade.

Harvesting Memories

With baskets bulging, laughter flies,
Collecting chuckles under the skies.
Wobbling pumpkins, a sight to see,
 Each one whispers a joke to me.

Apple cider spills, what a delight,
 Giggles pop out, oh what a sight!
While squirrels wear acorns like hats,
 Nature's a stand-up; how about that?

Whimsical Reflections

Mirrors of puddles, laughter in bloom,
A butterfly flutters and smells like perfume.
Chasing shadows, skipping along,
Who knew giggles could be so strong?

Pinecones sing as they drop on the ground,
Every note is a silly sound.
Rabbits in coats, do they write?
Jokes from the bushes, pure delight!

Alluring Echoes

In a world of wonder, where tickles reside,
Echoing laughter, a joyride.
Bouncing blueberries, round and bold,
Each one's a tale that's waiting to be told.

Chocolate fountains flow with glee,
Every splash's a reason to flee.
Sticky fingers and cheeky grins,
This is where the fun begins.

The Crush of Time

Tick-tock goes the clock, oh dear,
Wrestling with moments, sincere.
I tripped on yesterday's shoe,
And landed in next week's queue.

I spilled my drink on my plans,
A party with invisible fans.
The future slipped through my hands,
Like sandcastles made of bands.

Raft of Serenity

On a raft made of bubblegum,
Floating far from where I come.
With oars of chocolate, oh so sweet,
I paddle past gummy bear feet.

The waves laugh, a sugary sound,
While marshmallow clouds swirl around.
Lollipop fish swim by me,
In this calm, chaotic sea.

The Sweetness of Being

Life's a candy shop, oh what cheer,
I nibble on joy, never fear.
Chocolate rivers, licorice trees,
Sugar rushes, a vibe that frees.

Giggles bubble like soda foam,
I'm dressed up in a jelly bean dome.
Each day brings a fruity surprise,
As I dance under lemon pies.

Carousel of Thoughts

Round and round, my mind does spin,
On a horse named 'Where to Begin.'
With each gallop, laughs ensue,
As I think of the silly things to do.

A giraffe wearing roller skates,
Jumps on board, oh how it States!
We whirl with ideas instead of fear,
As cotton candy clouds draw near.

Beneath the Boughs of Introspection

Under branches thick and wide,
I find a seat where thoughts abide.
A squirrel steals my sandwich treat,
While I just sit in a comfy seat.

Sunbeams dance like silly sprites,
As I wrestle with my brainy fights.
Do ducks really have a sense of style?
Or is it just their quacky smile?

Sweetness in Silence

In moments quiet, thoughts collide,
Like bees in search of somewhere to hide.
A cookie crumbles without a sound,
Is it a snack if no one's around?

I grin at birds with tiny feet,
Debating if they still want to eat.
The sun peeks in, a playful tease,
As I wrestle with my busy bees.

Fruits of Reflection

I sit beneath a lopsided tree,
Wondering why bugs chase after me.
Do apples dream of being pies?
Or just find joy in sunny skies?

A breeze whispers secrets so sweet,
While ants form lines in a parade neat.
Do fruits ever argue about their fate?
Like, 'I wish I could be on a plate!'

Sweet Musings Under a Bough

Here I lounge with thoughts that sway,
Wondering if clouds want to play.
Do butterflies laugh at my dread?
Or simply float around my head?

The shade wraps me in comedic bliss,
As I wonder, what have I missed?
Do seeds whisper tales of old?
Or are they just waiting to be bold?

Blossoms of Thought

In the orchard, ideas grow,
With every breeze, they softly flow.
Nuts and fruit clash, what a sight,
Funny thoughts dance in pure delight.

Bumbling bees buzz round and round,
Collecting laughs from the ground.
While squirrels chat with acorn glee,
Misdirected plans in the tree.

Honeyed Evenings

As the sun dips low, shadows play,
Sticky fingers, oh what a way!
Dancing flames wink in the dark,
Jokes dripping sweet like honeyed spark.

Fireflies join in, quite the scene,
Buzzing jokes like a comic routine.
Laughter lingers as stars appear,
Underneath the glowing veneer.

The Taste of Serenity

Sipping nectar in the sun,
Every drop brings waves of fun.
Sour faces turn into grins,
Quips and giggles, where joy begins.

Savoring moments, giggly bliss,
Each chuckle—a delectable kiss.
While thoughts float sweetly, we agree,
Laughter's the fruit, wild and free.

Ripening Wisdom

Grown-up lessons dressed in jokes,
Wrinkles hidden in fruit-smoked pokes.
Silly tales from elder trees,
Whispering secrets in the breeze.

Each laugh a leaf, fluttering down,
A tapestry woven in this town.
Ripen the fun, let it expose,
Laughter blooms wherever it grows.

Juicy Reverie

In a grove where fruits collide,
Laughter spills on every side.
A pit rolled out, oh what a sight,
Chasing shadows, pure delight.

Sunshine drips like honey sweet,
Silly squirrels dance on their feet.
With every bite, a giggle flies,
Underneath the bright blue skies.

Summer's Sweet Reflection

A splash of juice upon my chin,
Look at that, I've done it again!
Sticky fingers, grinning wide,
As the fruit from trees takes a ride.

Sipping nectar, can't help but grin,
Each drop's a treasure, where to begin?
A frolic through this summer spree,
Who knew delight had quite this glee?

Whispers of the Orchard

In the shade, the gossip flows,
Branch to branch, the laughter grows.
"Did you taste that red delight?"
"Oh, I've dropped my snack, what a plight!"

The breeze brings chuckles, oh so fine,
As bugs join in, sip on the brine.
Fruits whisper secrets, giggle and sway,
Underneath the sun's warm play.

Nectar Dreams

In the twilight glow, I lay back,
With visions of fruit in a juicy stack.
Dreaming away, oh what a blast,
As I ride on waves of flavors vast.

Mischief bubbles, absurdity spins,
A parade of snacks, where the fun begins.
With every dreamy, juicy puff,
I laugh and think, is this enough?

The Heart's Orchard

In the orchard, giggles bloom,
Bouncing fruits escape their gloom.
Juicy jokes hang on each branch,
Funny faces in a dance.

Silly squirrels with silly hats,
Chasing shadows, playing prats.
Laughter echoes through the air,
As they tumble without a care.

Apples grinning, pears in glee,
Peeking out, as if to see.
Who will pluck them from their home?
With each bite, we laugh and roam.

Sweetness at Twilight

Under stars that softly wink,
Fruits invite us, pause and think.
Juicy whispers, sticky hands,
Sweet giggles across the lands.

Mango mischief in the night,
Jumping high, oh what a sight!
Ripe bananas slide and squeak,
As we burst with laughter's peak.

Twilight fruit are on the prowl,
Each one grins, and none will scowl.
With every bite, the world spins round,
In this sweetness, joy is found.

Autumn's Gentle Footsteps

As leaves turn and softly fall,
Fruits gather for a leafy ball.
Plums and cherries toss their puns,
Wrapped in hues of orange fun.

Cider spills with giggly cheer,
While pumpkins roll, don't come near!
Squirrels chuckle, nuts in hand,
In this vibrant, nutty land.

Fruits in sweaters sing delight,
Each a tale of pure jest, right!
As autumn dances with a grin,
We join in, let the laughs begin.

A Tapestry of Flavor

In a market bursting ripe and brave,
Colors weave where giggles wave.
Bananas chat with berries sweet,
Creating mischief, quite the feat.

Citrus laughs, all zesty bright,
As each fruit takes a silly bite.
Kiwi sings, a wobbly tune,
Underneath the smiling moon.

A cornucopia's playful show,
Each fruit joins, putting on a glow.
In this tapestry, we delight,
Sharing laughter, all through the night.

Moments in the Shade

Under trees, we laugh and sway,
Collecting dreams in a zany way.
A squirrel stares, quite bemused,
As we spit seeds, feeling amused.

Bold sunbeams dance upon our skin,
We trade tall tales, let the giggles spin.
With juice-stained cheeks, a sticky plight,
Wait, did I just swallow that seed tonight?

Second helpings turn the table round,
While ants have an unexpected mound.
We joke of picnics gone astray,
And laugh till dusk takes bright away.

The breeze carries antics from afar,
'Who tossed that pit? Was it you or me, star?'
In shadows of vines, we find our glee,
Come join this silly conspiracy.

Golden Hues of Memory

Bright sunlit tales warmed by the past,
We gather friends like sweet treats amassed.
With laughter crisp, and joy integrated,
Our memories blend, never outdated.

The fruit salad's dressed in stories tall,
Of mishaps and laughs we can't recall.
We debate who dropped what as time slips,
And relish the taste of our friendship's sips.

Golden laughter under dappled light,
Seuss-like antics take playful flight.
"Did we really think we'd dance on the grass?"
As the unplanned slip brings a good laugh en masse.

The moments we share, how sweet they blend,
In hues of joy, where the good times tend.
With every chuckle, the old times renew,
Memories grown chubby, just like our crew!

Choices Beneath the Canopy

Beneath the leaves where the mischiefs flirt,
We weigh our choices, and sometimes get hurt.
To climb or not, is the pressing debate,
While squirrels mock—'Get on with your fate!'

Shall we pick the fruit or play in the sun?
It's hard to decide when both look so fun.
Each berry glimmers, a tempting delight,
But risk slipping down adds thrill to the night.

Queries float like petals in the breeze,
'Is that the right pick? Did we miss some cheese?'
In decision-making, chaos can reign,
With us gaining bruises while laughing in pain.

As choices are made, we dance on the ground,
Savoring nonsense, let laughter abound.
In the shade we declare, our whims are a blast,
What's next on this journey? It's fun—hold on fast!

Savoring Tomorrow's Fruits

With baskets full, we dream in the light,
Of taming our futures, oh what a sight!
The futures we crave are sweet and so sly,
But what if tomorrow just makes us cry?

Plucking hopes from branches, we hum in delight,
Each glance toward the sky sparks laughter outright.
And when nature grins with a wry little tease,
We cradle our plans like a mild summer breeze.

Morsels of fancy dance on our plates,
As the jokes flow free from nearby tree mates.
Perhaps we'll find joy in the mess that we make,
Savoring giggles with each silly mistake.

The future's a feast, come share it with me,
Each slip and each trip embellishes glee.
Tomorrow will bloom, with a wink and a squish,
Delighting in growth like a whimsical wish!

A Cornucopia of Contemplation

Beneath the tree, we sit and munch,
Sipping ideas with a side of lunch.
Thoughts roll in like fluffy clouds,
Ideas burst out with giggles loud.

Juicy dreams tumbling from high,
Why do birds not wear a tie?
Squirrels plot in a theatrical way,
While we laugh at their wild ballet.

Each slice of fruit holds a tale,
Stretching our minds without fail.
Each bite's a burst, sweet and bright,
Offering whims that feel just right.

So let's dive into the absurd,
Tasting life with every word.
Under the shade, we play and tease,
Finding bliss in the summer breeze.

Juiced Thoughts

In the kitchen, juice drips down,
Thoughts get sticky, wear a crown.
The blender's loud, a chuckling mate,
Whirling ideas at funny rates.

Straws like wands, we summon glee,
What if cats could ride a bee?
Sip by sip, we ponder stuff,
Laughter bubbles; isn't it tough?

Pulp of wisdom in our cups,
Squishy fruits and silly hiccups.
Ideas dance, they twirl and whirl,
In this juiced world, it's a swirl.

Sipping slowly, sweet and soft,
With every giggle, our spirits loft.
Funny thoughts land on the floor,
Like a peach that wants to explore.

Under the Blossoms of Inquiry

Beneath the blooms, questions fly,
Like buzzing bees that taste the sky.
What's the secret to a good nap?
Do giraffes wear a little cap?

Petals flutter with every breeze,
Whispers of humor put us at ease.
We ponder why socks like to hide,
While the sun giggles, our faithful guide.

Each thought a flower, blooming bright,
Crafting laughter from pure delight.
With each tickle of the air,
Curious minds make quite a pair.

Let's climb high on this silly tree,
Where questions bloom and minds run free.
Under the blossoms, we shine so bright,
Chasing wonders into the night.

Lush Delays

Procrastination's a fruit we savor,
Chewing time with goofy flavor.
Why rush through the day's bright meal?
Laziness wraps us up in a reel.

A hammock dangles, inviting rest,
While plans sit idle, that's the jest.
Each lazy hour brings a new joke,
What if turtles could dance and smoke?

Serenity's a sweet little bane,
With every giggle, we play the game.
Whisking thoughts in a world so lush,
Cultivating humor; oh, what a rush!

So here's to delays that make us grin,
In a world so funny, it's where we begin.
Let life unfold at its own sweet pace,
And find joy in this delightful space.

The Essence of Sunlit Days

In a land where laughter grows,
Fruit hangs low, in rows and rows.
Sunshine dances on juicy skin,
Beneath the branches, giggles spin.

Squirrels wear shades and strike a pose,
With tiny cocktails, who knows?
A watermelon slice provides the shade,
While ants play cards—a grand parade!

In this orchard, joy is ripe,
Each smile plucked, a tasty type.
With sticky fingers, we munch away,
On a carnival of a sunny day.

Such flavors mix, oh what a sight!
Laughter echoes, pure delight.
Beneath the glow, we savor all,
In this land of fruity brawl.

Fruity Contemplation

Beneath the tree, we sit and muse,
On fruit-filled dreams, and silly cues.
A grape debate on who's the best,
While strawberries laugh, they're not impressed.

Cherries roll in, wearing a grin,
Claiming they're the sweetest kin.
While bananas slip and take a dive,
In this fruity world, we come alive!

Lemons frown, but join the game,
Adding zing to our silly fame.
With peachy whispers floating by,
We giggle loud beneath the sky.

A fruit parade, a vibrant show,
Where every twist brings laughter's flow.
In this orchard, mirth won't cease,
As we revel in this fruity feast.

Delicate Musings under the Tree

In the shade of branches, we weave our thoughts,
While juicy treasures down below rot.
A lime complains it's too tart to play,
But citrus jokes brighten the day.

Dabbing at sticky fingers and grin,
With every taste, we lose our chin.
Pineapple chunks debate their crown,
While apples roll, just trying to clown.

A sprinkle of laughter floats in the air,
As we sip on juice without a care.
In this fruity realm, we ponder fair,
Every giggle brings us closer, I swear!

We share our secrets, hushed and sweet,
As bees dance near—a buzzing treat.
Under the tree, life sways with ease,
In this fruity haven, hearts tease.

A Slice of Stillness

In a moment filled with fruity cheer,
A slice of laughter is all we steer.
With watermelon wedges stacked in a pile,
We take a break and share a smile.

Here, time pauses, draped in fun,
Where silly thoughts collide and run.
The puns fly high like kites on a breeze,
While juicy delights bring us to our knees.

Oh, the nectar of bliss in every bite,
As grapes offer a toast to our shared delight.
And in this stillness, laughter rains,
Fruity memories grow like sugar canes.

With every noise, a new joke takes flight,
In the orchard's fun, everything feels right.
A delicious slice of silliness found,
In this fruity fiesta of joy unbound.

Depth of Fragrance

In a grove where breezes dance,
The scent of sweetness takes its chance.
Bees buzzing loud, quite a chatter,
As I munch on fruit, what could be better?

A plump delight, it falls and rolls,
It's like a game that tests our souls.
I slip and slide on juice galore,
Oh, who knew fruit could be a chore?

My laughter bursts like cherry blooms,
As friends all gather, sharing boons.
Who knew that munchin' could cause such ruckus?
I blame the fruit for making us fuss!

With faces sticky and mirthful cheer,
We laugh till the sun begins to disappear.
In this orchard of jolly delight,
We ponder life 'til the stars are bright.

Calm in the Orchard

Under trees with leaves so green,
We saunter slowly, what a scene!
A picnic spread, all laid so neat,
With fruit that's ripe, what a treat!

But wait! A squirrel steals my snack,
With a cheeky grin, it makes its attack.
I chase it down, we both have fun,
This little thief just loves to run!

Laughter echoes, a chorus we share,
Between bites of fruit, we haven't a care.
Joyful moments, we savor the sun,
In this calm, we find we've won.

As twilight whispers, we share our dreams,
With laughter and fruit, nothing's as it seems.
A perfect day, with friends close near,
Life's quirks unfold, and we stand clear.

Blossoms and Serenity

The petals twirl like joyful sprites,
Beneath the sun, they dance in flights.
We balance fruit upon our heads,
A silly game, no worries, no dreads.

Each step a giggle, each bite a cheer,
As sweetness lingers, we draw near.
The challenge grows—who will beat me?
Oh, how this tree brings such glee!

With every stumble, we burst out loud,
In a world of green, we feel so proud.
Who knew serenity could be so wild?
Like laughing kids, we've all beguiled.

At sunset's call, we toast with zest,
To the orchard's magic, we are blessed.
Laughter and blossoms, a lively spree,
In this gentle bliss, we all agree!

The Golden Fruit of Thought

A golden fruit, full of surprise,
With every bite, joy multiplies.
We sit in circles, minds all ablaze,
Ideas tumble out in a goofy haze.

"Is it sweet? Is it tart?" we quiz,
Each flavor leads to a moment of fizz.
Thoughts get wild, as we take a plunge,
Who knew fruit could inspire so much funge?

Suddenly, a debate breaks out,
About the best way to dance—no doubt!
A fruit-fueled battle, we laugh and shout,
With every jest, our worries flout.

At day's end, with bellies full,
The golden fruit makes us all a fool.
With laughter ringing under the night sky,
We leave the orchard, feeling high.

A Symphony of Juices

In a garden where flavors dance,
Fruits debate their grand romance.
A berry boasted, sweet and bright,
While a citrus tried to steal the light.

Beneath the sun, a grape did cry,
Sipping juice, oh me, oh my!
A melon chimed in with a tune,
"Let's mix it up beneath the moon!"

They gathered round, a juicy crew,
With laughter sparked, they bubbling grew.
Each one felt their essence blend,
Creating joy that won't soon end.

So here's to all, the juicy cheer,
In every bite, we taste the sphere.
A banquet served, what a delight,
Our fruity game, a sheer delight.

Aromatic Journeys

Oh, the scents that waft and tease,
Bouncing lightly on the breeze.
Cinnamon and citrus swirl,
In the kitchen, watch them twirl.

Ginger hops with glee and spry,
While basil sings a savory sigh.
Rosemary rolls in with flair,
Spices mingle, do not care.

Coffee beans begin to dance,
Chasing dreams in a caffeinated trance.
Honey drips like golden rain,
Tickling taste buds, sharing the gain.

Let's embark on this wild ride,
Where flavors mix and worlds collide.
Aromatic tales to sweetly share,
In every dish, joy's always there.

Golden Hours and Reflections

As the sun dips low and bright,
Shadows stretch, seeking flight.
Lemonade laughs in a glass so tall,
Inviting all for a fruity brawl.

Underneath a shady tree,
Cherries tumble, wild and free.
Peppers punch with vibrant zest,
Each bite, a giggle – life's a fest!

Cucumber whispers with cool grace,
While radish spins in a silly race.
Together, they share stories bold,
Of sunny days when life unfolds.

Golden moments ripe and clear,
Juicy memories, we hold dear.
With laughter ringing in the air,
Let's toast this time, with love and care.

The Harmony of Softness

In the orchard, breezes sway,
Fruits sit snug, a cozy array.
Plump and round, they take their seat,
While laughter rolls from soft to sweet.

Fuzzy friends like to unwind,
Tickling each other—oh so kind!
A pineapple grins, all decked in spikes,
Playful banter with pear-like likes.

They sing of squashes and tender greens,
Creating scenes straight from dreams.
A giggle from a pumpkin, oh so great,
"Come join the fun, don't hesitate!"

So gather 'round, let's make a feast,
With every bite, savor the least.
In this harmony, young and old,
Life's fruity tales just waiting to be told.

A Touch of Sweetness

In the orchard, giggles rise,
Fruits in dresses, quite a disguise.
Tiny critters holding a feast,
Squirrel's dance, a comedy beast.

Leaves gossiping in the breeze,
Whispering tales 'bout clumsy thieves.
A bear in shades, trying to blend,
But all he steals is laughter, my friend.

Juicy jewels hang on the vine,
Winking at folks who sip their wine.
With every bite, a silly grin,
Life's a romp, let the fun begin!

So let's rejoice in this delight,
As fruits beam under warm daylight.
Each chuckle sweetens the sun's glow,
In this merry orchard, let joy flow.

Serene Musings in Bloom

Petals chatter with a wink,
Bumbling bees begin to drink.
A flower sneezes, bless its heart,
Who knew blooms could be so smart?

Underneath the sunny sky,
A ladybug gives a wink, oh my!
With tiny glasses perched on nose,
She reads the news, the garden knows.

A dandelion with big dreams,
Wants to be a star, or so it seems.
It laughs and twirls, then takes a leap,
But winds just blow the seeds to sleep.

In this garden, laughter spins,
Each blossom wears a grin, it wins.
Let joy and whimsy fill the air,
In this patch of magic, without a care.

Murmurs of the Orchard

Under trees, whispers abound,
Pears gossip, laughter's their sound.
Funky fruits roll on the ground,
Even apples join with a pound.

A crow in shades struts with flair,
His fashion sense? Beyond compare.
He caws with joy, no hint of frown,
While mischief hides in every crown.

Plums and peaches plan a race,
All in good fun, just a chase.
With one big leap, oh what a sight!
But they trip and tumble, pure delight.

So when you roam through grove and glade,
Join the laughter that won't fade.
For nature's humor, wild and free,
Is the sweetest part of the jubilee.

Wisdom in the Ripeness

In the orchard, wisdom grows,
Funny tales the fruit tree knows.
An old fig jokes, 'I'm wise with age,
But watch the youth; they're all the rage!'

Grapes in bunches laugh out loud,
Getting tipsy, feeling proud.
With every sip from nature's cup,
They giggle as they bubble up.

A peach once said, 'I'm getting soft,
But in this life, I still lift off!'
With every bite, flavors burst,
In fun's sweet essence, we all thirst.

So gather round, share a cheer,
With fruits so ripe, the merriment near.
For wisdom lies in folly's dance,
Here in this orchard, take a chance!

Peeled Layers of Imagination

In a world where thoughts can dance,
Ideas bounce at every chance.
A fruit of wit, so soft and bright,
Sprouting laughter with delight.

Peel away the silly layers,
Sticky giggles, merry players.
Each thought a segment, juicy fresh,
Spritz of whimsy, oh so mesh.

In gardens where the dreams collide,
Silliness is our trusty guide.
With every layer, jokes unfold,
A treasure chest of fun untold.

So slice the fruit, enjoy the cheer,
In wacky thoughts, we persevere.
With each new layer, laughter grows,
Unraveling life in comical rows.

A Walk Among Dreams

Strolling through a witty haze,
Each thought's a wild and silly phase.
With each step, a laugh will sprout,
In this monkey mind, there's no doubt.

Twinkling stars with cheeky grins,
Chasing tails of ancient sins.
Where nonsense thrives and giggles reign,
In this dreamscape, we're all insane.

Hopping clouds and skipping beams,
Whispers play like cartoon dreams.
Every breeze a belly laugh,
Turn the mundane into artful gaff.

So join the stroll, let loose the flair,
With every step, shed every care.
We wander where the silly thrives,
Among the thoughts where humor drives.

Blooming Soliloquies

In a garden where laughter grows,
Every petal a joke that flows.
Tickling toes with playful jibes,
Nature's punchlines, oh so bribes.

Watch the flowers wiggle with glee,
Spinning tales beneath the tree.
Each bloom a quirk, a jesting cheer,
A riddle wrapped in a fragrant sphere.

Buzzing bees with puns to share,
Jiving through the fragrant air.
Silly whispers on the breeze,
In every laugh, the tension frees.

So cultivate a life of jest,
In this field, we're truly blessed.
With every bloom, a story knits,
In blooming moments, laughter fits.

Shadows Under the Tree

Beneath the leafy canopy,
Giggles float so light and free.
Where shadows play their silly games,
Tickling toes, they call our names.

A squirrel's tale, a zany mime,
Nature's jesters, all in rhyme.
Wobbling branches, playful claps,
Wrap us tight in laughter's wraps.

A world beneath the gnarled limbs,
Where thoughts can blossom, whimsy swims.
In the rustle, we hear the tease,
Of giggling winds that aim to please.

So gather 'round this laughter tree,
Let the shadows set us free.
In every chuckle, joy does swirl,
For life's a sketch, a funny whirl.

Gentle Ruminations

In a garden where laughter grows,
Squirrels dance in striped clothes.
Bumblebees hold a buzzing debate,
On the joy of a sweet cake.

Up in the tree, a parrot sings,
Claiming to know all the things.
A rabbit nods, takes a bite,
His ears flapping with delight.

Sunshine spills like lemonade,
While the ants form a parade.
They march in line to the picnic spread,
Stealing crumbs, a nod to bread.

A clever fox in a top hat,
Recites poetry to a fat cat.
They trade jokes while sipping tea,
Oh, what laughs, just wait and see!

Bountiful Dreams

In a field where buttercups sway,
The cows tiptoe through their play.
Chickens croon a silly rhyme,
While the rooster steps in time.

Clouds are cotton candy fluff,
Twisting into shapes so rough.
A giraffe does a jig around,
Causing giggles; oh what sound!

The moon wears sunglasses at night,
Stars join in, what a sight!
A turtle races, slow yet spry,
While fireflies blink in the sky.

Underneath the comedic tree,
Squirrels argue over glee.
They tumble down, but with such style,
For laughter lingers for a while.

Daylight Reveries

A pig in sunglasses takes the stage,
Telling tales of a new age.
His audience roars with delight,
As he juggles apples, what a sight!

The sun winks at a lazy bug,
Who rolls over with a shrug.
Ladybugs cheer on the side,
As the beetles join the ride.

Dandelions sway in a dance,
Each fluffs up for a chance.
A breeze teases the daisy crowd,
As laughter bursts, remarkably loud.

Chasing shadows in the grass,
A hippo trips, oh what a class!
With a splash, he lands with flair,
In the stream, without a care.

Beneath the Canopy

Under branches where dreams collide,
A tortoise hosts a wild ride.
His friends on leaves like boats,
While the chipmunks sing high notes.

A wise owl narrates a tale,
Of a squirrel who chased a whale.
They giggle at the thought of it,
As the rabbit tries to knit.

Butterflies in tutus fly,
Twisting and turning in the sky.
Each flap sends the beetles twirling,
In a delightful dance, unfurling.

As the sun dips low to rest,
Creatures sigh, feeling blessed.
In this realm where fun runs free,
Each moment feels like a jubilee!

Fragrant Echoes

In a grove where sunshine beams,
Chubby cheeks hide silly dreams.
The fruit above begins to swing,
As squirrels dance and robins sing.

Jars of laughter fill the air,
With mishaps here and joys to share.
One brave bite, a juicy dare,
Splatters laughter everywhere!

Bouncing, giggling, such a scene,
Honey drips, a sticky sheen.
Friends collide in fruits galore,
Nature's jokes, we can't ignore.

As summer whispers in our ears,
We taste the fun, we drown our fears.
In every bite, a silly tale,
With every laugh, we set our sail.

A Lullaby of Summer

Beneath the boughs, the twilight hums,
The drummers beat of buzzing bums.
A napkin hat on a ladybug,
Twirls like it's found a cozy rug.

Chasing shadows among the trees,
Ants in line say "please, oh please!"
Fruits hang low and wiggle down,
While giggles echo all around.

A split peach here, a feather there,
Jumpers jump, unaware of care.
Swaying like the breeze in flight,
We share our dreams under moonlight.

Silly songs drift through the field,
To all our secrets, now revealed.
Each note a treasure, laughter skies,
In this lullaby, joy never dies.

Soft Blush of Emotion

Blushing skin beneath the sun,
Tickled noses, oh what fun!
A giggle escapes, a wild chase,
In this sweet, warm, fruity place.

Juicy dribbles, silly slips,
Caught in laughter, not in grips.
Soft and fuzzy, colors bright,
Even bugs join in our light.

The sun pokes through the leafy lanes,
As laughter bubbles through our veins.
Each moment bursts with joy and cheer,
While summer dances, drawing near.

So grab a bite, let worries go,
In this funny show, we grow.
The soft blush of our delight,
Turns every day into pure light.

Melodies Beneath Leaves

In orchards green, a songbird flits,
Tickles all with its funny skits.
Leaves dance lightly, join the fun,
While shadows play beneath the sun.

Fruits like marbles roll around,
With giggles erupting from the ground.
A quirky charm fills every nook,
Where laughter flows like an open book.

Oh, tender bliss of summer's cheer,
Each bite brings friends so near.
Chasing each other, toe to toe,
Our joyous melodies steal the show.

So sing and sway, let spirits rise,
Each fallen fruit a sweet surprise.
In the heart of nature's tune,
We flourish like a summer bloom.

Lush Epiphanies

In a grove where laughter grows,
Beneath the weight of fuzzy shows,
Fruits giggle as they sway with grace,
Tickling leaves in a cheeky race.

Bugs in hats, they dance and prance,
While sunlight casts a golden trance,
Each drop of dew, a tiny joke,
Nature's whimsy, awfully woke.

With every bite, a funny face,
Juices drip in a wild embrace,
Citrus quips and berry cheer,
Life's a fruitcake, hold it dear.

So come and join this merry spree,
Where laughter hangs like a ripe decree,
In the shade of trees, let's be absurd,
For even fruits can sing a word.

Sunkissed Thoughts

Sunbeams chase as shadows play,
Bright ideas in disarray,
Silly squirrels with tiny shoes,
Plotting antics in shades of hues.

A garden tea where laughter brews,
Crumpets served with giggles, too,
Butterflies in a waltzing flight,
Their wings aflutter with sheer delight.

Thoughts sizzle like the sun-kissed ground,
Each one a quirk, a funny sound,
Hypnotized by a honeybee,
I think it's laughing back at me.

Let's raise a glass to whims anew,
In this garden, our dreams accrue,
With every sip, a chuckle's spun,
Our minds bloom bright under the sun.

A Garden of Stillness

In a garden where silence sings,
With petals flapping like little wings,
Worms wear goggles and sunblock, too,
While daisies gossip in morning dew.

The hedgehogs throw a fashion show,
In their finest spines, they steal the glow,
Ladybugs in polka dots dash,
While frogs croak jokes in a make-believe splash.

Roots tickle toes beneath the dirt,
In this stillness, there's humor to flirt,
A cabbage nods in wise intent,
Reciting puns, oh, what a scent!

Amidst the blooms, a jest runs wild,
Nature's laughter, eternally styled,
So find your peace in every laugh,
In this quiet space, we find our path.

Gathering Light

In a field where beams conspire,
Chasing shadows with eager fire,
The sun spills gold like honeyed cheer,
While clouds throw shapes, so crystal clear.

Illuminated gnomes in hats so tall,
Drawing ever closer to a sudden fall,
With every step, the daisies giggle,
A symphony of quirks that make us wiggle.

Each ray a laugh, a playful jest,
Tickling whispers in the nest,
Colors merge in a playful flight,
A gathering of joy, a pure delight.

So let us bask in the glowing hue,
With every sparkle, there's something new,
These moments shine, so funny and bright,
Together, we'll gather this warming light.

Warm Breezes and Lost Thoughts

A breeze blew lightly past my nose,
It carried whispers, tickles, and prose.
I thought of lunch, but what was that?
A fried tomato? Or a brisk chat?

Dancing leaves flaunt their leafy sway,
While squirrels rehearse their acrobatic play.
I forgot my goal, lost in this show,
What was I doing? Ah, who really knows?

The sunbeams played hide-and-seek,
With shadows casting a crafty sleek.
My thoughts were a game of hide-and-squeak,
I laughed aloud, "Hey, don't be a freak!"

In this funny realm of nature's charm,
I often find myself snuggled, warm.
A little confused but full of glee,
For life's just a puzzle, don't you see?

Nature's Soft Discourse

The grass whispers truths in a rustling way,
While bugs gather round to laugh and play.
I leaned in closely to hear their chat,
But sneezed and startled a nearby cat.

The flowers giggled in vibrant hues,
As bees buzzed by with their sweet little tunes.
I asked a daisy for some advice,
It replied, "Just bloom, it's surprisingly nice!"

A breeze combs through the tall, wild grass,
Where thoughts float by like clouds made of glass.
I chased after one, but it sped away,
Leaving me chuckling at the nature ballet.

In this garden of laughter, I find my way,
With every odd twist of a verbose play.
For humor blooms where life's carefree,
Just listen closely, and you might agree!

The Color of Reflection

Mirrors of water catch thoughts that swim,
A splash of color, a whimsical whim.
I leaned too close, my face got wet,
"Oh, what a sight!" I laughed, with no regret.

The clouds held conversations, soft and gray,
While I pondered if I'd lost my way.
A duck quacked loudly, a quizzical sound,
Did he just question this circus I found?

Colors danced like ballerinas on stage,
As silly thoughts pranced free to engage.
I painted my worries with vibrant cheer,
With every splash, nothing seemed unclear.

In this artwork of life, I find my muse,
With each swipe of laughter, I simply refuse.
To take it too serious, what a bore!
Let's splash on joy, and then add some more!

Silken Juices of the Mind

Thoughts drip and slide like syrupy sweet,
As I ponder the morning and all of its treats.
Muffins are magic, but what's in my head?
A mélange of thoughts, where chaos is fed.

Sticky ideas cling to my brain,
Like honey to fingers, a sweet little stain.
I try to wipe clean but the laughter persists,
As I juggle my thoughts like some bizarre twists.

With each juicy notion, I take a bite,
Some flavors are funny; some take flight!
I mix up my dreams with jelly and toast,
And giggle at the visions I love the most.

So here's to the flavors each day imparts,
With whimsical thoughts that tickle like arts.
A feast for the mind, silly grapes of delight,
Let's savor this banquet, both day and night!

Boundless Respite

In a world where fruit can chat,
One told me, 'Life's a cake, not a brat!'
I laughed so hard, I lost my hat,
While dancing with a curious cat.

With every giggle, the sun did shine,
We tossed around all thoughts divine.
Between the trees, we sipped sweet wine,
And pondered what it means to dine.

Was it the pie that made us grin?
Or the silly games that we jumped in?
A field of joy, we're sure to win,
Chasing laughter with a goofy spin.

So here's to bites of crazy cheer,
In fruit-filled fables, have no fear!
Join the jesters, let's draw near,
For in this glee, we're all the seer.

The Taste of Daydreams

In dreams of cream, where giggles swirl,
I took a sip from a marble pearl.
"Is that a drink or a dancing girl?"
With giggle fits, my mind's in a whirl.

A spoonful of chuckles, a dash of fun,
With every nibble, we're far from done.
A sprinkle of mischief lies under the sun,
And laughter becomes the number one.

Nibbling clouds and tasting the breeze,
Floating with joy was so much ease.
In this silly space, we do as we please,
Inventing new games like cherry trapeze.

So let's raise our glasses, toast the unseen,
Where dreams are as sweet as jellybeans green.
Life's a banquet, a comedy scene,
In a realm where silly is always keen.

In the Garden of Whimsy

In a garden where giggles bloom,
A flower declared, "I'll be your costume!"
With butterflies gliding, avoiding the gloom,
We danced on petals, a colorful room.

The trees wore hats, the bushes sung,
While we spun tales of the young and the fun.
Giggles and snickers, we haven't yet spun,
Under the rays where dreams are begun.

With frolicsome rabbits who tell silly jokes,
And wise old turtles who trade in hoaks.
Amidst all the folly, the laughter provokes,
In this land, all logic gently chokes.

So let's unwind in this quirky space,
Grab a handful of joy, quicken the pace.
For every good laugh is a warm embrace,
In the garden of whimsy, we find our place.

Luscious Thoughts Unfold

In a kitchen where giggles grow,
I mixed up dreams with a dash of show.
The oven bubbled, unleashing woe,
As marshmallows danced in a silly row.

A cookie monster snuck in to snare,
While I pretended not to care.
He took one bite, and up flew my hair!
"Why so serious?" he asked with flair.

With every mix, a story would sprout,
A rainbow cake that made us shout.
Each layer of laughter, a joyful route,
In this slice of life, we never pout.

So gather around, with cupcakes galore,
Fill our plates with sweetness and more.
In flavors of friendship, let joy soar,
For luscious thoughts open every door.

The Nectar of Thought

Sipping juice from an absurd cup,
A thought dripped in, and I hiccuped up.
Was it sweet or just sticky? Who can tell?
My mind's a fruit salad, swirling so well.

The bees buzz louder as I chase a bee,
They laugh at my pondering, just let it be.
In the orchard of nonsense, we twirl and spin,
Thoughts like cherries, are they lost or win?

Each bite of reason is a bit of delight,
A slippery notion that takes to flight.
I chuckle at quandaries, hold my head high,
For humor's the nectar, oh my, oh my!

A twist of the brain, a spoonful of fun,
In a field of laughter, there's room for everyone.
So come, take a sip, let your worries depart,
For the nectar of thought fills the belly and heart.

Whispering Orchard

In the garden where giggles grow tall,
The trees tell secrets, oh, do I fall!
With whispers of sweetness in every breeze,
Fruits share their tales, and I'm weak in the knees.

A wobbly branch drops a tiny delight,
I catch it mid-air, it's a comical sight.
Laughter erupts from the roots to the sky,
As squirrels roll over, just passing by.

Bleeding laughter from berries so bright,
They sparkle with joy, oh, what a sight!
I munch on the giggles, they tickle my soul,
In this orchard of whimsy, I've found my role.

So come stroll with me, through this laughter spree,
Nature's a jester, won't you agree?
With each silly moment, let worries be sown,
For the whispers of joy are never alone.

Juicy Contemplations

A squish and a splat, oh what a thrill,
Thoughts dribble down like a smoothie spill.
Every juicy ponder is coated in cheer,
I snack on my dreams, they're not far, they're here.

The sun's shining brightly, the view's quite absurd,
As I munch on ideas, they fly like a bird.
A slice of confusion may wobble and dance,
Though donned in bright laughter, they lead me to prance.

With watermelons claiming they know all my woes,
Miraculously wise in their seedy repose.
I ponder in play, with each fruit in my hand,
Finding giggles in musings, oh isn't it grand?

Crumbling clues like cookies, they scatter about,
In the realm of delight, there's never a doubt.
So bring on the juice, let's twiddle and tease,
For juicy reflections are certain to please.

The Essence of Sunshine

Under bright rays, on a splendiferous day,
I search for the essence, just to play.
With laughter like nectar dripping from trees,
I chuckle at shadows, they dance with the breeze.

A daft little critter with a twinkle in his eye,
Hops in my lap with a very sly lie.
He claims he's the king of this fruity land,
I giggle and nod, give his silliness a hand.

The sun's got the giggles, it tickles the air,
As butterflies giggle in a whirl of flair.
I chase the warm rays, let my thoughts take flight,
In the essence of sunshine, everything's right.

So come join the fun in this zesty embrace,
A cloud of giggles, a bright, silly space.
With every warm beam that playfully shines,
The essence of joy—for all of mankind!

Contemplative Harvest

In a field of yellow hats,
The fruit can play a game,
It rolls away like laughter,
And calls us all by name.

With baskets strapped on shoulders,
We hop and skip with glee,
But missed the fruit still giggles,
As it rolls beneath a tree.

We chase it through the haystacks,
A dance of pure delight,
Each slip and slide a chuckle,
As sun fades into night.

And when the day is over,
We ponder our grand quest,
But the fruit just winks and whispers,
"You surely did your best!"

Delicate Dreams in the Grove

In a grove where whispers chatter,
Breezes hold a peachy chat,
The leaves all start to giggle,
As if they know what's that.

Hanging low, the round delights,
Dangle in a blissful sway,
They taunt with fruity chuckles,
While we try to have our say.

We swing around in circles,
And trip beneath the boughs,
Just then a fruit declares loud,
"I'll never share my vows!"

The laughter floats like petals,
As we tumble in the grass,
Each dream is bright and fleeting,
In this grove where moments pass.

Ripened Reveries

In a garden ripe with giggles,
Each fruit is dressed to cheer,
They prance about in sunlight,
Whispers tickling ear to ear.

One jolly red is boasting,
"I'm juicier than you!"
While yellow ones are planning,
Their own fruit parade too.

We toss the ripened treasures,
As if they might just dance,
But they roll away in laughter,
Breaking fruit's sweet romance.

With juices flowing freely,
The laughter fills the air,
We dream of fruity stories,
As we breathe in the fair.

Slices of Serenity

In a bowl of creamy colors,
Fruits lounge and take a nap,
Each slice is full of secrets,
Wrapped in a juicy wrap.

We take a bite and giggle,
As sweetness floods the day,
The fruits break into chuckles,
While we munch our cares away.

A lemon's sour protest,
With bitterness in sight,
Yet everyone just winks back,
"It's fun to be polite!"

So we slice and share the moments,
In flavors bright and bold,
Each bite a funny story,
In sweetness to behold.

Elixirs of Mindfulness

In the garden of thought, I sip and sway,
Chasing thoughts like butterflies at play.
A sip of dreams, a dash of delight,
Giggles and snorts with each mental bite.

Juggling my worries like juggling balls,
They bounce and they tumble, crash down the halls.
With every blunder, I burst into glee,
Who knew self-reflection could ever be free?

I brew up a potion of silly sighs,
A splash of laughter that never denies.
Between rooibos and chai, I find a groove,
Dancing with wonder, I'm ready to move.

To pause and rejoice in this zany zest,
Is to find in each moment, it's truly the best.
With elixirs so fruity, what more could I say?
Life's just a chuckle when taken this way!

Vibrant Cadences

In a whirl of colors, thoughts spiral and zoom,
Singing songs of madness inside my small room.
Noisy ideas with feet in the race,
I chase them all down, can't find a trace!

With rhythms so merry, they tap at my door,
Each line a giggle, who could ask for more?
A pun or a jest dances right on the beat,
As laughter rings out, making life sweet.

My mind's a big circus, all clowns and delight,
Juggling my cares, oh what a sight!
With vibrant cadences ringing so true,
I find joy in madness, and sip it like brew.

Each thought's a balloon, floating high in the sky,
I pop them with smiles, oh how they fly!
In this funny parade where thoughts don't retreat,
I laugh like a child, and it feels so complete!

Garden of Whispers

In secretive corners, ideas take flight,
Bumbling around like bees in the night.
Whispers of nonsense tickle my ears,
I giggle at thoughts that defy all my fears.

Like gnomes in the shadows, they dance and they prance,
Each fleeting idea leads to a chance.
With every soft chuckle and wink from the sky,
I find joy in nonsense, oh me, oh my!

Petals of laughter fall gently to ground,
In the chaos of thoughts, tranquility's found.
Rustling secrets, they tease and entice,
A garden of whimsy, oh isn't it nice?

In this patch of delight, in this playful spree,
My heart tumbles wildly, twirling with glee.
For life's a sweet riddle, wrapped up in dreams,
In this garden of whispers, nothing's as it seems.

Warmth of Reflection

A mirror of giggles reflects back my face,
In this warm little bubble, I find my own space.
With each chuckled thought that dances and twirls,
I sip on my wisdom, add sprinkles and swirls.

Like cozy campfires that flicker and gleam,
I roast up my troubles, an absurd little dream.
As shadows of laughter weave in and out,
I ponder the zany, there's no room for doubt.

With warmth wrapped around me, I sway and I smile,
Each silly reflection is worth every while.
Finding humor in moments that seem rather bleak,
Turns life's little quirks into joy that's unique.

So gather 'round gently, let silliness flow,
In this warmth of reflection, we let laughter grow.
In the fabric of life, in threads that we weave,
A tapestry of joy is what we believe!

www.ingramcontent.com/pod-product-compliance
Lightning Source LLC
Chambersburg PA
CBHW062109280426
43661CB00086B/399